THE JOURNAL CHARLES B. WHEELER POETRY PRIZE

JUNE IN EDEN

ROSALIE MOFFETT

MAD RIVER BOOKS
an imprint of
THE OHIO STATE UNIVERSITY PRESS
Columbus

Mad River Books, an imprint of The Ohio State University Press.

Library of Congress Cataloging-in-Publication Data

Names: Moffett, Rosalie, author.

Title: June in Eden / Rosalie Moffett.

Description: Columbus : Mad River Books, an imprint of The Ohio State University Press, [2016] | "Winner of the 2015 The Ohio State University Press/"The Journal" Charles B. Wheeler Poetry Prize"

Identifiers: LCCN 2016036323 | ISBN 9780814253847 (pbk. ; alk. paper) | ISBN 0814253849 (pbk. ; alk. paper)

Classification: LCC PS3613.O366 J86 2016 | DDC 811/.6—dc23

LC record available at https://lccn.loc.gov/2016036323

Cover design by Regina Starace

Text design by Juliet Williams

Type set in Adobe Janson and Frutiger

9 8 7 6 5 4 3 2 1

for my mother and father

CONTENTS

ACKNOWLEDGMENTS

Thank you to the editors of the journals and anthologies in which these poems, or their previous forms, appeared: *32 Poems*, *AGNI*, *Blackbird*, *Boston Review*, *Colorado Review*, *Day One*, *DIAGRAM*, *Gettysburg Review*, *Gulf Coast*, *Indiana Review*, *Kenyon Review*, *Mid-American Review*, *Narrative*, *Pleiades*, *Ploughshares*, *The Poetry Mail*, *Tin House*, and *West Branch*. "The New Trees" was featured on *Verse Daily*, and "The Way it Works" was featured on *Poetry Daily*. "Biology" and "A Certain Eden" were anthologized under the titles "Instar and Eclose" and "Knecht with Nature" in *Gathered: Contemporary Quaker Poets* (Sundress Publications).

Thank you to Marcus Jackson for selecting this book, and to OSU Press and *The Journal*.

Thank you to Mary Szybist, for her role in what might be called the beginning; Marianne Boruch, for her attention and wisdom; to Don Platt, the Purdue faculty and workshop, especially Greg Allendorf, Lindsey Alexander, and Lizzy Peterson. Thank you to Stanford University and the Stegner Fellowship for the freedom to write many of these poems, and to the faculty: Ken Fields, Doug Powell, Simone Di Piero, and Eavan Boland. Thank you to my Stegner Workshop for their intelligence and commitment to poetry, particularly to Ari Banias, Allison Davis, and Corey Van Landingham, whose advice remains indispensable. Thanks to the Bread Loaf Writers' Workshop and my fellow waiters and staff, especially Sam Ross for his look at this manuscript.

Deepest gratitude to my mother and father, Stacia and David Moffett, for letting me have the world and teaching me to see it.

And to Jacob Sunderlin, with love.

REVISIONS

All over town, trucks reach out
their three metal fingers, grasp trash bins,
lift them in an arc. I am out walking, placing

myself somewhere in the city's fractal
of receptacles, when I see a little dog
in the mouth of a big dog. The word is

throttled, though I struggled for days
to think of it. What's that joke—*What's
black and white and read all over?*

And you know the answer is *A newspaper*
because you've heard this one before.
But then you're told *A nun*

falling down a flight of stairs and this
is how the world works
itself out from under you. *Red.* The inside

out, the language all shifted. What had been
harmless, the morning dove,
looking dark and sorry, all of the sudden

that someone's died. The context, it turns
out, is at the mercy of the interior.
You can forget even the smallest things

—a vowel, invisible, a bright drop
of blood—wheel the world
around them.

WHAT IT WAS

The tomatoes were uneven, yellow-pocked. It was August.
  I was chipping their spots into a bucket with the tip of a knife.
    The day, its sky and lull, was like the hotel pool

we woke up one morning to find some drunk
  had driven into. I was saying *What will it do,*
    to know? And my father, *Nothing.* And my mother

was up in Spokane, finding out. Gold-green blaze
  and that side of the tomato never got sweet. It was stink bugs,
    sticking the fruit with their straw-mouths. It wouldn't be the first time

she'd been told she was going to die. *What it is, is a little poison*
  the stink bug lets slide back in to the tomato. This,
    which might've been the very edge of what it was

she didn't say in the year after she drove home,
  hairpinning into our dry canyon with their words—*A disease*
    where you stop talking, stop breathing—spreading

inside her. If she said anything she said, *Hardship is good*
  for the vines. Unscrewed the soaker-hose. *They're too happy*
    to set fruit. I didn't believe, at the time, in happiness

that could hurt you and so watered and watered
  and they grew like a forest to the ceiling, only a few
    tomatoes you had to fight to find.

BIOLOGY

I know metamorphosis turns
a kaleidoscope

into a caterpillar and then into a gypsy moth
with a furry mouth. I've learned

some things. To mimic injury

the plover drags a wing
in the dust. The lure

of a wound is always enticing

away from something
smaller, more

vulnerable. Inside what looks
like a dress,

gauzy white silk, the tent
caterpillars

set to ruining
the tree.

TAXONOMY

The hurricane with its whorl-eye—drunk
cyclops, feeling the land

for people—had a man's name and looked
small on the Weather Channel, kneading its white way

up the coast. She, much smaller and not appearing
on the news, had a woman's name

meaning *resurrection*. Eye to her microscope,
she made imperceptible cuts,

opened the tiny world of the snail brain.
When injured, snails—slow, droll, miraculous—

regenerate. Do a thing that looks like learning,
like forming in the womb—*re-member*—what translation

could be made for us, what remedy, she'd wanted
to know. Wondered it even as the ground moved,

as her bike flipped. The hurricane cut the lights
in the hospital. A similar, dim blue, her concussion

refused to undo itself. Human brains do not renew.
No rewiring, no sweet grit to hinge

to the word *pear*, none of her assiduous knowledge—
the Latinate taxonomies collected, pinned

carefully in the mind. Of it all, only one
round term surfaced, perfect

and complete: OPERCULUM,
meaning *little lid*, with which the snail shut itself in.

WEATHER

Clouds gather. On TV a prizefighter
has his storm, and evening spins me
in its darkroom door.

What do you end up doing
in the avocation of sleep? *I'd like*
some kind of break please. Sudden rain

blooms under the streetlamp, a light-cone
of seeds. *To be pelted a little,*
I'd like that, I think. The boxer's eyes

are a precise kind of shuttered.
Make a fist, the end of which resembles
his swollen ear. *I like that idea,* shut up

like that, to be in a clenched hand,
a hug machine
when you need that wrapped feeling

but still can't stomach
anyone near.

SPASM

He tells me what's wrong
  with her makes her

move all night as if she's a seed pod
  inhabited by the larva of a moth.

What my father really says is *I'm sleeping*
  next to a Mexican jumping bean

but I look this up and receive
  the image of my mother opening

down her middle, soft
  brown moth there, twitching its fringed wings.

This makes the only sense of anything
  I've thought yet. The language

of neurology is pictureless
  as a ceiling. I leave

the encyclopedia open
  to the illustration of the almost-circle

the larva chews in the pod's husk—only
  to seal it shut with silk

before going about the business
  of transformation.

Later, the new moth, mouthless, will push
  through the trapdoor, enter

the world of air. If my mother
  imagines death, she hasn't told me

what it looks like.

THIS WORLD, ITS WEATHER

Not dawn, but the microwave
doing its mysterious molecule rattling
with a cup of coffee. The hum-comfort and glow—

up this early, I can't help it if I see a dead ringer
for the sun there, next to the sink. For a time,
I was a twin. I waited in something I imagine

as a planetarium with the one who was
not me, who would disappear. This was before
my brain began to take

its automatic notes, so I felt nothing
that I know of when the partition went up
between us. I was assigned to this world, its weather

and oceans and dark 6AM kitchens, my body
well-suited to transmit messages: how spring came all
of a sudden with its mania of crocuses, how it burnt

just now, the coffee pulled from its star. I fire
my circuitry, feel each thing
the way a fax machine would: brilliant

as it passes through. Somewhere, I have a sister
circuit, wired in mirror image. All night I understand
the data to be hers.

THE BATHROOM WALL SAYS *WOMEN*

were the first 3D printers. So I imagine the machine
sucking up the souls of dead objects—i.e., the gun

thrown in the sewer, the deck chair collapsed
and splintered on the freeway—and offering
them a home in the home-miracle of a prosthetic ear

or an ice-cube tray, the way my mother did
with me, who had been—don't you feel this?—something

else, a dog or a bear or a snake before I was me,
coming into being layer by layer. At the urinal
he realized it was his phone he cradled in his palm

when my friend read, at eye-height, *Why are you looking up here?*
The joke is in your hands. It comes as no surprise

that everything is flying towards one point, like gulls
converging on a scrap of something we can't quite see yet—
last bit of humanish real estate. By which I mean, yes

I wonder what glitch it would take to glance over
and find, printed out, twins. And yes, you can choose your lover

on your new phone and my new phone talks at some length
to me. Old news, all this, and even comforting. My mother, though
she made me, can't make hers work, can't make it close

the distance between us, like those snap-back strings
that prevent your lighter from being pocketed

by some absent-minded smoker about
to walk away with something that is yours, even
though you only bought it, and could buy another.

DELAYED FLIGHT

I love the word *terminal*, how it conjures
a huge window

to taxiing planes. To planes taking off.
That clockwork

access to sky. Sorry, I'm sorry
to twist the airport

into morose metaphor. Here,
a joke, to make up for it: two

muffins are in an oven. One
says to the other, It's getting hot in here—

and the other says, Holy shit!
A talking muffin! I don't know why

this is funny, except, how silly to need
to be reminded to turn to you

and say, *We're in this together.*
The right thing to say, and how close

it is to being true.

HOW TO RETURN

Galveston, Texas: helmetless, my mother
unaware, was lifted or cradled or cars
she did not recall wove around her.
The hurricane buckled some houses

into the surf, filled the town like a bathtub.
Everyone evacuated while she waited
in the hospital, wondering what
was the word for that, again? To empty a town—

The names of her children straggled back to her
one by one while, on the top floor
of a Dallas hotel, we watched Inspector Gadget's
fingers turn into flashlights. We knew we fled

in heavy traffic, a storm, but not that we had been cast
from our mother. Anyone can leave
through a door. I wish I'd known
to leave through a wall, breaking

cartoon-like, a perfect body-
shaped hole. This is the only way,
isn't it, to know how to return exactly
to the same place as the same, exact person.

I FOUND A KNIT OF BRANCHES IN A CAVE SHAPE

I found the shape the body makes when it flinches
at the explosion of two pheasants
from the underbrush. It obscures me.

I curl up in it. I make believe
at homesteading. This is a good way

from the town where I was born,
the town with the barber and his plastic
lit-up nativity scene and the woman and the man

on the sidewalk in front of the Circle K
who are breaking

their last cigarette in half
under a billboard with a sausage McMuffin and a McCafé
and the words *True Love*.

Mary, socket by her knee, glows. I can never remember
whether it is a *praying* or a *preying*

mantis. The kneeling, the ambush—I made mistakes
when I was little
about which hand shape to make

to pretend I had a gun
when we played those games

where you needed one.
Now, I make a church: my pointer fingers
are the steeple, my thumbs, the doors.

I point my church at a coyote
and fire.

JUNE IN EDEN

Then I went into the garden
and forgot all about it. Some spider
mums, some slug half-buried

in a strawberry. *I have this thing*, my mother
says, *with memory.* The thing rings or is left
on high. The thing dissolves

as if it had never been seen
at all, makes of itself a question
answered and answered. Objects behave

like the tree: every morning more
candy-colored pie cherries. *Because Rosi, don't you love*
this Eden—its beetles, its blooms, all waiting

to be named. Elsewhere, the world
has discoveries. Impossible phones, drones,
new kinds of war that keep

changing the maps. She though, can't hold
a map in her mind—*I broke*, she says,
my cartographer. Everything outside the garden

can do as it pleases with computers, etc.
Here, there are things coming into being
all the time. There are so many

strawberries, as yet unmarred,
the plants sending out their runners,
covering up the garden pathways.

THE ONLY PARADISE

Turbines spun under water and this is why,
when I climbed at night certain hills, there were lights

bunched up in the distance. In photos of the orchards,
of the steamboats loaded with stone fruit, men worked

land they'd named after themselves. For years, I wondered
why *imminent domain* sounded like a territory

that was just coming into being
but meant one that could be made

to disappear. My mother was the one
who'd wanted it, the canyon that had been

emptied of people and filled with water. It was she
who said, *If you can't see it, you make a guess*

based on context. This, about homophones,
but she was looking around her—the hillsides

hauled up against the sky, and behind them, the dam—
as if to take stock. This was when we were digging rocks

out of what was to be the new garden. She was looking
at us as if down from a great height.

This was when she'd lost only a few words,
had replaced them right away

with other, similar ones. We were not *ready*
anymore, we were *prepared.* When the land was seized,

they picked up and moved, whole, the post office
but left the houses. The river rose, swallowed.

Memory is the only paradise from which we cannot be driven
it said on the cover of a blank photo album I found

it in myself to scoff at. Though that was later, when I knew
about her brain, how it looked—even the doctor said—like a city

at night with small, black power outages.

THE NEW TREES

Cell towers can be hidden inside an artificial tree.

The new trees rise up and up, fingering out, one cell
in a cellular network. They do everything
the old trees did: listen, collect our discarded breath,

transmit it new into air. We need them. We take them
ugly and make them hidden: crown of fronds, green
more ever than evergreen. And then we talk to them

the way we used to talk to dolls. They weren't quite right—
too light, never blinked—but they were ours
and knew our language the way babies never did.

HYMNS

This leaning in
to look closely at the ditch-leaves. Their solace
of rest. I sing like this

singing is a shell
I'll leave after I'm done using it.

Rest is a break sometimes
and a remnant
on the floor other times

after the dress is all sewn.

OUTSIDE PASCO

Sunset, gas station, stuporous smell,
     I give back the psychedelic blue-eyed Virgin Mary
        key chain, the key to the cement
bathroom whose cool tile is kind
     of like prayer, I think
        that's what I'm supposed to think.
One-story hotel, one blip on the highway that splits
     my state in half. Dust, fuzz of mariachi, forest
        of electric towers, this is that Washington.
High school soccer teams speak Spanish,
     scrimmage all August against each other
        and evening. Against being
one mote in the optical illusion
     of trellised rows, a tiny body
        in a pinpoint of light—light that stays put
even as you drive by if you train your eye on it right.
     The Columbia River is combed out
        into vines, aisles like lines on an open palm.
You never feel how it closes around you
     if you are just passing through.
        In the Oasis RV park and hotel, people sleep
through the hot part of the day. Sleep,
     an empty highway shimmying
        up into blue—the land so flat,
most of what's there
     turns out to be sky.

INTERSECTION

It's as if all the roads between a thing

and its name disappeared. Texas 87 washed
itself into sand, entirely. Our flimsy rented house

was intact, the little yard leaping with fleas, just

as we left it. She was home. She looked the same,
but you could watch her feel

around for a word, as if along a wall for a light switch.

We waited at stop signs: empty intersections,
blank, whole minutes passing.

The brain has to beat down new paths.

Uncanny: Highway 87 never was rebuilt—
too close to the gulf, to the rising water

to be patched. And now *She is*

losing her marbles, is how my father puts it.
His way of not looking. (Of looking

so at it.)

We have in our hands
what the MRI made of her brain:

something like a sliced loaf of bread.

I examine the intricate map of white lines
where I must, in some form, reside.

I don't immediately see

any soft spots—The Specialist,
pointing, hopeful—*where we look at memory.* But I feel

very soft, or I hardly feel at all.

COMFORT

Yes, I would have you
believe that I didn't put my sadness on
one leg at a time. But I'll tell you now,
we start out the day the same: right leg, left leg,

then the shoes. Remember that odometer
you gave me? I held it like a disembodied heart,
ticking up the numbers with my thumbs
until—the best part

—they all turned over to zero. We love
the things we love because they work
like machines, are fixed, are unaware
of their advantage.

HAND-SIZED EXPLOSIONS, THE PEONIES

are blood-colored, are flouncing in the wind. Some dark tumble,
too, of clouds. The world gesticulates wildly: a girl
who has crashed her car, waving her arms
on a country road. I like perfection

—the row of aspirin in a plastic blister pack,
the tilt of Jackie Kennedy's head in every photograph. I like it
when things hold still. As a child in a museum
I looked straight into the bison's eye. Of course, I knew

even then that it was glass. The stare, nonetheless,
was real. Was animal. Almost all
packaging presents an argument about scale.
There is a reason the frosted flakes are enormous.

There is a reason people are afraid
of the ocean. We suspect it's not there
to show texture, to take us and give us up. Like most,
I love the *mock*—mock turtlenecks, the mock-orange tree

hanging its white blossoms over the road.
What is enough to be named for the real.
My lipstick is peony-dark.
The car in the ditch has one wheel up, turning

a little. I hold my arms
in the air. I do not wave them—

ROSALIE RUTH MOFFETT

Sometimes a twin absorbs her sibling
in the womb. My mother bled a little,
so maybe I did this. I knew even then

what sympathy was: another discomfort.
Nonetheless, they named me Ruth
which is a kind of compassion

nobody wants anymore—the surviving half
of the pair of words is *ruthless*.
My eco-terrorism handbook says

some plants come back forever,
through anything. I've planted some stands
of bamboo where they'll grow through the floor

of the new strip mall.
Like Ruth, the Moabite, I desire
to be something that can't be

gotten rid of easily. Loyal, she gleaned
in the grain, and maybe something went on
with Boaz on the threshing floor in the dark

one morning. All this I read in the Bible,
which is a kind of handbook
that helps people name babies. I miss, I guess,

the one who should have been Ruth, whose name
I stole and wore. I took a little of her
as collateral damage.

REMEDY

Sometimes I stand on the sidewalk
near the street sweeper.
I think it scrubs what people like
to call personal space.

It feels ok.
Ladies with bright lacquered nails
are on TV, excited
about home remedies: club soda

or toothpaste or lemons, etc. In real life
that almost never works.
In real life, I tried to get the stain out.
Then it began to look

like such a person—I could make out
two eyes, a kind of mouth. *You,*
I would say to it, are hidebound.
You are a stubborn bit of the world

on me. And then, *Are we friends?*
On TV, the ladies don't address this. Never once
is the topic Miraculous Home Remedies
For The Unaccountably Alone.

FILL IN THE BLANK

Is warehouse to
house as werewolf is to wolf? Am I in a pack, now
what with the dark, what with that bellyish

yellow moon, of homes

gone toothsome? Someone's general
decree: things shall be scary
at night. Things shall be boarded up. This shall be

to that thing as this is

to _____? I am to him as he is to—yes, I am
uncomfortable when I see the pear
grown inside the bottle. In the test

question, I confess, I am the pear. We are

trained to fill the blank. No relationship
is without a vacant sidecar. Not even, especially not
the lonesome. (Here, my lamp-shadow,

taking over the empty street.)

Eyes are to the soul as windows
are to the ___TV___. The best shows I've seen, I've seen
walking the dog at night, which is to say

I've seen in the lit blue interiors

a kindred spirit, fallen
in love with whatever
we live in that is bottleish,

whatever we fill.

ARTICULATION

Botany.
   a joint or place between two parts
where separation may take place
spontaneously, as at the point
of attachment of a leaf. If you find where
in yourself what you want
to say leafs out
into words, you might
snap it off.

NEW EVIDENCE OF WATER

It was a mistake, perhaps,
to pick the most loyal breed of dog.
The day, after all, is always breaking

into two or more pieces: war,
postwar, etc. We occupy ourselves,

the dog and I, with the news
of our incredible luck: our tiny orbit
at the Goldilocks distance from the sun

where water is neither frozen
nor steam. Everything else

is an *uninhabitable zone.*
Which must be what I'm looking at every time
I look into the distance, or into the laptop

which is a kind of distance, its own
telescopic view

not only into space, but also
of a gutted tank, of a woman in a green dress
climbing out of a pile of cinder blocks.

The buildings on Earth seem to be either
flattened or huge, depending. In other news, some horizon

has a nick in it, which means there may
have been water, once, on the moon. On TV
a boat parts the great Pacific trash vortex

only for a second. I think we must
want to leave

except gravity so loves us we can't
help but love the world
we made and all its shadows.

One follows me around
like a dog.

QUESTION

—even after they said no said we don't know
what it is this small region all gone

strange that governs her oh words
and reflexes both but no it's not the one

we thought when we said dead inside
of a year when we said the one where you stop

talking eating breathing though
for the record what was the tally

of nights and could she feel it the bit of space
the world made for her to be in

closing I think yes many nights she made
dinner went to bed got up let her dog out

she stood still at the end of the hallway
where there was a mirror

instead of more hallway—

NOISE

Some dogs, addicted
to fetch, bring you the worn ball, drop it
        at your feet. Over
and over, this thing, still
mouth-wet and warm. Hers, though, no
interest in that, sits, tips
        his head left, right, cocked-up
ears at the rise and fall of noise. Words

though the aphasic misses them, are just
one piece. You cannot lie
the neurologist claims, to an aphasic: *They are like dogs,*
  sensitive. The expression gives
        it away. But to have it
be just sounds, a voice. Just something
going on in the air:
        the magpie or the jake-brake
of the grain trucks descending the grade, the rhythm
of the woodpecker in the poplars—a feel

  to it, almost a color. To have that
be all. After all, conversation
while grubbing in the garden, walking the fields, was
  unnecessary,
shed like nice shoes she never wanted
to wear. Her hand

  now on his head, now
resting on his shoulders. No neon yellow, no obligate
object to cycle back and forth
        across the room, across the field, not
with this dog. It had always been

easier with animals, hadn't it. Wasn't it
going to be even easier
        from now on.

PRAYERS

I address the terns. Really,

I address my own hand, curled into a horn.
I tip it up. I say

I am caught floor-side of the trapeze net.

For the flightless, there is very little
satisfaction. The birds practice

their routine, performing as black bits

in a sink after a man has shaved.
The sky plays the sink. Here, as always,

the beach is littered with stupid things. Empty water

bottles. Shells of such delicate intricacy,
they make me feel like dieting. Most of the time I don't

notice though, because there's something distracting

about my phone. *Let me up with u birds!*
is a text message

I send up into the sky. I can't

help it: what a flimsy little voice
I have.

SAFE

The city, of course, never sleeps though it drowses
like a shark: eyes open, the big part of its brain

turned off. My truck was shark-like
in that I was the little sparked awake part of its brain—
turning the wheel, deciding directions.

I drove and the street appeared, each streetlamp
proof of a little bit more. The Bank of America gleamed,
fortressing in its bulletproof glass. Elsewhere

entirely, it seemed, my arms and legs
were working—the intelligent orphans—together.
In that sense, one could trust things

would turn out all right when they really ought
not to. What prayers one says
for the yolk of oneself. The bank

was admirable—something about vaults
with complicated doors, the shiny barriers
to its indomitable bank-heart,

the way the big thing just hunkered
and refused to move, admitting so few
to the important rooms.

A resolution: be more bank-like. But all the lights
turned green. Not luck, just mechanical
ushering—toward somewhere,

some other guarded heart,
bigger and more chambered.

THE WAY IT WORKS

is not that I am half her and half
my father, quite, so it's not true
that I am destined to half of her

totem pole of doctors—
or exactly half her body's refusal
to go through this world assembled

in a way anyone understands. My brothers
don't question this, that they are separate
as moons. They don't look

like her. They orbit, tall, black-haired. They reach,
lift things down from the top cupboards.
Me, though. Who am I but her

creation, clicking around in all her old
high heels? *Listen, who knows*
where this comes from. And you, you

must have inherited your brain
from your father. But I have her arm
in mine so she won't stumble because

that's what the medicine does, undoes
the balance calibrators. I hold tight. I am careful,
as we walk, to watch where she puts her feet,

which means I am looking at our legs
stepping in time with each other,
like someone next to a mirror.

ON EMPTINESS

A cop car sirens by, starts up
      the foxes warbling and yelping
into the night, chorus like the twirl

      of red-blue lights spinning the air
we've been breathing all along, not
      remembering it was full

of police-wake, detritus of voice, thinking
      it was tasteless like clear plastic
around spring water or pills

      coated so when swallowed no trace
is left tongue-side. I polish the illusion
      in my fortress of luck

that each breath is unsullied, that the poem
      can be born, warbling, from the air
pristine—but watch the news as it makes an arrangement

      of violence apparent.
Whatever is built, I know, is not built
      on solid ground. See how cement

poured into an anthill makes available a monument
      —colossal, complicated—
to hidden emptiness. See the science-fair carnation,

      its white frills full of the red
food coloring dripped into its vase-water.
      The poem can't take

a breath, can't expand
      without drawing up into it the holes
drilled into the world

every time a boy, cold hands
holding his toy gun, head full of who knows what,
    looks up, hears, for the last time,

who knows what.

POEM WITH A FORKLIFT IN IT

The lung is a mosaic

of specialized mouths.
Each passes air down

tiny fingered trees to the place where oxygen is
fed into the smallest of ATMs.

Then the CO2 is pushed out, and then
I don't know where it goes.

Some try to say it goes into plants, but we need that
unknowing.

It's best not to keep track
of the most personal transactions: for instance, money

spent like a hemorrhage
after my brother drove a forklift

on the highway and the car he saw for a second
in the mirror was the car that hit him.

For instance, exchanges involving various words,
the result of which is silence. Exchanges

involving molecules
of breath and of fragrance—because

once a thing is lost, it is wrong
to keep looking. The man

who had a pea lodge and grow
in his right lung knows

what it's like, letting something live
inside you.

ANATOMY

The desert is surprising, a tissue sample
seen under a microscope: all those sunsets.
The ovary slide, the uterus slide.

Headlights, skin. My inadequate openings
are always framing things
out of the picture. The jackrabbits turn

their narrow faces and leap off the road.
In Las Vegas there are no girls
only *girls* with the hugest of eyes

and some faces
appear and reappear
behind hot pink phone numbers

on the sidewalk. I am in the light
of the neon, watching
through the watching side

of a two-way mirror. Five dollars
gets you one minute to see inside her
the way the microscope would

expose whatever was hidden
if you shut one eye right. Shut one eye.
Sit still. She is all sunsets.

All close-up and postcard and longed-for,
like how the slides are
never believably part of a woman.

A CERTAIN EDEN

I believe the landscaping
truck full of tree limbs
with the bumper sticker that says *Trees don't bleed*
because I believe in limblessness—

in the painless beauty of that
move toward cordless,
and then cell.
My iPhone is a small room.

It arrived without umbilical cord. Branchless,
doorless. I want this isolation.
I want just a trunk
the size of my grandfather's cigarette tin

to put everything in, no hassle
of lineage. The dog wags its cropped tail
anyway, I've noticed. I've noticed
they made the garden into a perfect line

of small pruned box-bushes. On every
cut, there are little yellow-sap topazes
like my birthstone earrings.

FALL

The birds eat the apples
off the apple-heavy ground.
Cold, snake-slow,
we roughen up the brush
the way a drunk comes on.
I bird-call my *bourbon*
bourbon bourbon and you
bastard, birdseed smile.
We fire, we while, we forage
and sleep. The season put the robins
in the breeze, put the bird-smell
in the air. The leaves never fell so
everywhere as they did in the forest
where they fell. On the path: the geodes,
broken open like bank safes, riched us like nature
always promised to. To the forest, the cold comes
oftener, the cloud and the crow, quicker.
We come and go, our preternatural jackets
all colored weird.

PLATINUM, GOLD, SILVER, BRONZE, CATASTROPHE

—The Affordable Care Act Menu

Because everything is caught
in winter's chokehold, I hold a heat lamp
over the water dish, its ice
lit unto precious metal, pocked
by the chickens who peck brainlessly
any shiny. Now, the marble,
put there to glint, to make the ugly
just-shipped chicks drink their water
by accident or die, is trapped at the bottom.
Tired, I roll my wrist, shine the light
over the slatted walls and resume
my alchemy. Later, maybe, I'll ask who it is
who practices their divination in the red
and blue shapes spun across the wall
by an ambulance, whose taxonomy is it
that spans the galactic distance
between a woman in the middle
of nowhere, falling, breaking,
two ribs on the rim of a feed bucket—
that is to say, the ungovernable open
mouth of the future
—and *bronze*. But now
I am busy directing
warmth, freeing up the water
kept in its ice.

THE FAMILY LIVES ON A FARM

The family is five: the girl, two boys, the mother,
and the father who sinks inevitably
to the bottom of the list. Most mornings,
an indigo bunting can be seen somewhere
in the orchard. The family depends on the mother

to remark nice things such as this.
The family sorts fruit: perfect peaches
here, earwigged and bruised ones over here. They eat
the latter and sell the former. The family doesn't mind
the heat and has enough money.

When a hen dies and is put in a trap in the sun
to ripen and lure a raccoon, the family
will admit to feeling both for the chicken
and like her. The father, especially, sees
something wire-like around him. Time

whetting a stone, a metal glint. Always
the boulders have been there, surfacing like whales
in the ground broken for the garden, the cellar. But that
always—sometimes it gets bad. His grip
on the forgetful landscape, loosening. And then

the father becomes like a small black hole
in a chair at the table. The family leans toward it, they can't
help it. The father is a clingstone, and each
of the children has a dark little peach pit
you might see if you split them open.

RADIOGRAPH

Forget atoms
and their empty rooms.
Forget what we thought we knew

about space and the Double Dutch
of the genome. I know. Built like an ornament,
here is my body, the receipt:

an expensive x-ray. I cracked
open my fortune cookie, a brown delicate
pelvis, and the message

was generic: Luck & Patience.
I hadn't wanted to look
into the windows

of my own house,
but there it was, my bowl
of bone glowed and glowed.

THE YEAR

As with the frigid patches of water I was forever
finding myself in and then kicking
out of into the rest of the river, the year
waited with its invisible holes. Home
was a house that was unchanged
except that it was. Some recalculation
had taken its place. The dogs dug tunnels
under the maple, tracked the world in
on their claws—a little grit
underfoot, a bit of the cold inner-earth, it was not
helping, not hurting. There was my mother,
still my mother, in the doorway
or the yard. There she was, holding out
the camera she'd just used to photograph me, the little me
contained inside it—*Take it. It's yours.*

THE SUMMER THE COLLIES

died and were buried beneath fir trees,
    I had two kinds of apple: red and red-yellow.
I had a three-legged aluminum ladder, a bucket, a wasp's nest
    the size of my fist. I fit between
the branches, filled, first my hands and pockets
    and then the bucket. A wasp with the face
of my oldest dog stung me twice. It takes a long time
    to leave. My father's green bulldozer will break down
in the purple-headed thistles some August
    and then stay and stay there. A tractor outlasts
a person. It's never worth it to haul it away.
    There are monuments, in the country, everywhere.
If I talk too often about wasps it's because they're inescapable.
    They'll be under the hood in no time—here, no emptiness
goes uninhabited. I always want to put Christ's heart back
    in his chest, like returning a jar of jam
to the cupboard. I make the bruised apples into sauce,
    ladle it hot into jars. *What is sown as perishable*
is raised imperishable—a joke I make
    to myself about the buzzing soul
of the bulldozer, existing here on earth
    long after it's died, as something venomous
and intelligent.

WHY IS IT THE MORE

I see of the world—heavenish
periscope of technology—the less
I can imagine God
                    intervening. Isn't it right to think that
given the whole thing at once,
we'd make out
                    some pattern we've been so far
too small to see? Flying out of Spokane,
the hills I grew
                    up in become doubtless
ripples, left behind by some giant
iceberg. That's what
                    I mean. To see the hand of the giant.
I'm sure there is someone
close by to tell me this
                    is ill-guided. This hope, this wrong
way to go about it. That no
matter what you think
                    you see you never
grasp the scope of what we're doing
to each other—
                    or undoing, or praying in our colorless
prayers. That is the muffling of being
small and human
                    and prone to peace
of mind. I don't understand why I give myself lectures
like this, the someone
                    I've imagined nearby for this sole
purpose does not look like any god
I know or one
                    that shaped an earth.

LONG DIVISION

It's almost autumn. It's almost human
the way everything changes into Ghosts
-and-Candy from Back-to-School. Costume switch
of deciduous packaging. The young mothers
standing at the legs of the play structure
have the faintest of crow's feet. They discuss
eye cream and TV and the war
that's been doing stuff for years
now, for the whole life
of a fourth grader. The topic shifts
to standardized tests. No one
insists we need to relearn long division
in this context. But remainders,
repeating decimals, those little pieces
left over after everything else has been divided,
they march on and on. They mean something
different now, don't they?

THE OBSERVABLE UNIVERSE

What a meager galaxy there is
in this vending machine cinnamon roll,
that metal spiral that turns to free it. Who knows
what else is out there.
They canceled the space program
and the universe is expanding wildly
—into what? I eat the center
and toss the rest: breakfast, a sacrifice
to Terminus, the God of borders. *Now, let us pray*
that the horizon, that lousy line
we've been waiting in, will end
up somewhere other
than where we started.
What a terrible morning this is, whirling
breakneck through space,
queasy with the view from the bus,
no cords to pull, stop requested, please
driver, somewhere beyond, where they have better
coffee, more perfect drugs.

RE: GRAND THEFT AUTO 2

How do i get to the country redneck places in gta II, i die and i can't find it anymore.
—recent questions, gta.wikia.com

Sex, your shadow, a really good
tangerine—some things are forever
lost when you die, though not the rednecks.

Drive NW and you'll find them in Redemption.
Their pickups are parked outside of Disgracelands,
that Elvis bar where the jukebox flips the days over

like pancakes, and never takes requests. You'll realize
after a while that the music just plays in a loop.
A dog in Argentina has visited his master's grave

every day for six years now and no one knows how
he even found the cemetery. That's real life, it was
in the news. Somewhere else,

is the dog's master, looking around
from the top-down, 2D game-view. Life seems to go on
in the hereafter—but it's different. He's still trying to learn

the new controls for his car. He doesn't know yet
that it doesn't really matter if he crashes,
if he crashes over and over. So he drives carefully.

Sometimes he tries the ESC button, just to see. If you see him,
you should tell him that he can go to the mobile home park
where the rednecks run the car crusher, or to the church

where the neon sign flickers from JESUS SAVES to U SAVE
but he can't go home and he should stop
looking for the edges of the game.

LOVE POEM

I carry a sawzall and a cell phone,
a small jar of oxytocin.
A little boy addresses the grocery-store
coffee grinder: *Hello, Robot.*

Hello child, hello miniature human, you freak me out.
O, but that faux-rolling thunder of the produce misters,
those little mechanical robins
newly over the celery—O how real
we want things to be. The bus has its voice

-recorded messages for me:
5th and Madison, 6th and Madison, leaving
fareless square—I open my jar
and refresh my wrists and neck and look around
for somewhere to write my name.

All night the buses run their pink lights.
Their confetti upholstery. I take my arms

with me everywhere: mid-winter
doll-weight. A heart is cut into
the pleather of the seat, no initials.

PUNCTUATION

The sea birds in their little black bodies
   crook into the kinds of sky-apostrophes
that make a contraction, or is it
   a possessive. One or the other. It seems important

to get that straight. The loss of a vowel strikes me
   as sad, though contraction is a kind of marriage,
a one-ing of flesh. In the mash-up the *o* disappears
   from *I can not*, makes you say it faster: *I can't I can't*—O

the unseen mouth, the little gape we take
   from our words, it seems important.

THE BEACH WAS A GIANT FIELD

of vision something tugged
at the edge of: a lollygagging kite. I was in

a pink swimsuit, tiny, I shook
my film canister of sharks' teeth. A nothing

noise, like the universe
        expanding faster, faster
than we thought. Kite-fishers use wind to cast out
far beyond their boats—
    isn't that reassuring

when two pieces get yoked together:
the word to the word, the fish, hooked and yanked
into air. I feel around for the feeling

of things coming together, for whatever
  is at work
       when heat smudges
the difference

between boat and ocean. Three pelicans
skim the breakers.

One twists and dives. The beach is pocked with crab shells,
  scallop shells, one eye
and one rubber strap from a pair of yellow goggles.
      Pieces. Isn't there at least one distance
that's closing? Tell me there is
    an invisible fishing line

hooked in me. Show me how lightning
    fuses the sand into glass.

TENSE

This is always
what they leave out

when they teach you the rules
of time and language: memory

is an absurd present
tense. Perpetual: you shield your eyes

and I run your chainsaw through driftwood
which sparks, opens, reveals

a white-striped river rock. Trees, like people,
swallow incredible things—i.e., *Time*

heals all wounds, or *Discard nothing
and you won't be discarded.* It's true,

you will be forever
collecting things

to say, to hold
you down.

PASTORAL

I bury the skunk
and poke stale waffle cones through the fence.

Watch the chickens peck them off. The rooster bleeds
from his skunk bite, hangs back.
I shovel up potatoes and ants and tiny white eggs

roil out. There is a frantic regathering of progeny.
There are lots of birds.

The sky is a huge sky stuffed with white fluffs. Don't pretend
you would love life in the country
if you really have no idea. The days crank themselves

through that contraption that cores and peels apples.
They come out the other side
empty, the way every time you dig a hole

there's never enough dirt to refill it,
even when you're burying something.

THE JOURNAL CHARLES B. WHEELER POETRY PRIZE